William Wray has
simple principles of
Tutor at the School
and is presently writing course material and
books which explore the themes to be found in *New Life*. He lives in London.

By the Same Author

The Book of Reflection

The Book of Decision

The Book of Spirit

Venus, How to Discover the Spirit
of Love in Everyday Life

NEW LIFE

TRUE VITALITY AND INNER PEACE

A Systematic Approach to Self Discovery

WILLIAM WRAY

Watkins Publishing
London

This edition published in the UK in 2002 by
Watkins Publishing, 20 Bloomsbury Street,
London, WC1B 3QA

Cover design by Echelon Design
Cover photograph © PhotoDisk
Designed and typeset by Echelon Design
Printed and bound in Great Britain by NFF

British Library Cataloguing in Publication data
available

Library of Congress Cataloguing in Publication
data available

ISBN 1 84293 061 3

www.watkinspublishing.com

CONTENTS

INTRODUCTION

Who would want to pass through this life without any real understanding of its meaning?

Who would want to be at the mercy of events, rather than being in command of life?

Who would want to have their health and happiness undermined by stress?

Would we not rather make of life something creative and satisfying?

New Life leads you on a path towards self-knowledge, certainty and peace. It employs a systematic method that is utterly transformative.

Enrich your experience
Possess the present
Empower your purpose
Escape stress
Find your strengths
Harmonise emotion
Clarify your thinking
Secure success

SELF-REMEMBERING

At the heart of *New Life* is a simple practice of Self-Remembering which allows the reflections that follow to be properly understood. Follow the method step by step, ensuring that you have reached each stage before moving on to the next.

1 Come to stillness.

2 Let go of the concerns that are at present possessing your mind.

3 Bring your body into view, and allow physical tension to dissolve.

4 Simply look – colour, form, light, space: and listen – sound, silence.

5 Rest in the awareness of all that is around you.

6 Become conscious of the beauty of this present moment.

Use the practice regularly. Make it part of your day. Return to it whenever you remember, not only in the quiet of your own home, but wherever you find yourself. Use it to claim back your life from all the concerns that normally possess it. To practise this in full a little time is needed, but even fleeting connection has its merit.

REFLECTION

In the light of self-remembering, turn to the following twelve themes. Each theme has a short introduction that briefly explains its nature.

Choose a theme that is appropriate to you, and draw from that theme a reflection that touches you immediately.

Allow it to rest in mind, returning to it throughout the day.

Carry *New Life* with you as a constant reminder.

Your Essential Power

What is this power that we possess, the energy to take on life, our inner strength, that force that makes us what we are?

We know we are alive, certain of our identity, and yet we seem to be changing all the time. We seem to be constantly under the sway of some passing whim, mood or emotion. We are perpetually possessed by the situations we meet. No one would be false to themselves willingly, and yet life has a way of drawing us in and encouraging us in the habit of forgetfulness. And the more we forget the less energy we seem to have, and the less freedom.

Self-forgetting would of course be far less of a possibility if we had a clear idea of who we were in the first place. We feel certain we know, but maybe there is more to us than we suspect. It's not for nothing that self-discovery has long been considered a central aim in life.

Use the reflections found in this chapter to encourage a connection with your own essential self. Discover the power that creates your individual life and your own true destiny.

To find your vitality, give it.

Throw yourself into life with abandon.

Generosity of spirit is a wonderful thing.

And so is Self-Remembering.

Use them both in equal measure.

Work for inner contentment and stability, regardless of the circumstances you meet.

Every time you're carried away check to see how far you've gone.

Then return to the real you.

There is a map of the journey,
and there is the journey itself.

By all means use the map, but not
in place of the journey.

Humanity is bound by a common bond.

In experience that bond is discovered not so much by trying to get rid of all the differences, but by allowing those differences to connect with their common source.

Recognise the common source, both in yourself and in those you meet.

*Remember that even the darkest
shadow is cast by light.*

*Rather than living in the shadows,
look to the light.*

It's the power we all possess.

Use it or let it run down.

Is it possible to be infected by the mood of the times?

When you appear to be something you know you're not, check to see if this is the real you or something in the air.

If you find that you are meeting the same old situation in the same old way, look out for the usual clusters of thoughts and emotions that have somehow claimed your identity.

True wealth lies within.

To escape poverty,
it's there you should look.

Nothing is more central to any experience than the consciousness that grants us that experience.

Learn to rejoice in the evidence of that consciousness, whether it be in response to the radiance of a distant star or the opening of a child's eyes.

When you feel your own vitality,
acknowledge the consciousness within.

*What are you doing with this huge
power you've been given?*

Human vitality is lost without wise use.

Truly in Touch

E verybody wants to be in touch or to keep in touch. When we are out of touch we can never quite get it together, and when we lose touch we lose something of profound importance – our friends and those we love. We may even feel at times that we have lost touch with life itself, and it's then that the alienation begins, and nothing has much meaning any more.

Yet, despite all this, lying at the heart of our perception of life is the consciousness that allows for connection of every kind. Without consciousness nothing could be seen or understood. To be truly in touch we must first come to an ever deeper recognition of our all-empowering energy, the very thing that gives vitality to life. When we acknowledge that, the divisions disappear.

With awareness of the abiding presence of our inner power, we become more in tune with all that is around us. What arises is the harmonisation of the inner and the outer, and the recognition that our fragmented lives, which can easily be experienced as so much separation, division and conflict, may be made whole and complete.

Through the use of the reflections in this chapter and the practice of Self-Remembering, keep continuously in touch with your own centre of strength and calm, the integrating power we all possess.

When you're feeling isolated,
go out and greet life.

Connect with whatever it is
that comes your way.

Give it your attention.

Touch whatever is in front, regardless of
how you think or feel about them or it.

*There's a joy to be discovered in doing
simple things with care and attention.*

*Discover that, and true artistry and
intelligence will be the mark of all
you do, however simple or complex.*

Communion means coming together as one.

*Inner communion is about returning
to your essential self.*

*To live in the knowledge of that
encourages connection of all kinds.*

Remember your friends.

Keep in touch.

Don't think that they're not interested.

*Your own enthusiasm will
soon kindle theirs.*

*Constantly return to the common ground,
the place where friendship is shared.*

*Find enduring satisfaction not so much
by being ruled by desire, but by entering
ever more deeply into that which
grants true satisfaction — your own
centre of stillness and certainty.*

Keep in touch with that at all cost.

Life is shaped by our minds.

Look at how events are formed by
the way you meet them.

'Cosmos' means 'the universe as an
ordered or harmonious whole'.

Constantly return to the cosmos within.

Fall still and find the underlying
factor that balances your nature.

Pause for thought.

Be reflective in your thinking.

Connect with the depth and stillness from which thought arises rather than worrying away on the surface.

Constantly return to here and now.

*Make conscious connection of mind
with the senses.*

*And when imaginings draw you away,
constantly bring mind back.*

In the seemingly imperfect nature of things, the underlying perfection remains in constant attendance.

You can get in touch with what's right for right now, by operating from that.

The Gift of Yourself

What does 'the gift of yourself' really mean? Is it true that in giving we receive?

There is this impression that we are isolated beings each with our separate consciousness, that we possess life for a short time, and that at the end of our time we lose this consciousness and leave this life.

As isolated creatures we are left to fend for ourselves. We acquire. We protect. We fear to lose. All this is believable but only from a separate point of view. There is, however, a problem with this way of thinking.

Experience tells us that there is no satisfaction to be had out of life when it is lived in isolation. What must be discovered is that, without making a continuous offering, the happiness we seek in acquiring and possessing is an impossibility. It is only in giving that we receive anything of lasting worth.

With every gift made, no matter how small, there must be a step out of isolation towards the unity that binds us all. And the principle of love insists that a deeper connection with another involves a deeper connection with ourselves. It's only in our own depths that we discover the source of real satisfaction and lasting happiness.

Use the reflections found in this chapter to dispossess yourself of the separate state of mind. Use them to discover another way of looking at life and, by seeing differently, be different. Become who you really are, and in the process give of yourself for the benefit of all.

Ask yourself what you might offer the moment rather than what you can take from it.

Count your blessings, and the next time you find yourself bewailing your lot learn to value those things that habit makes you overlook.

What is 'food for thought'?

*In every situation, seek the finest food,
and serve the finest food
with a generous spirit.*

Give yourself the chance to shine and in the process offer others their chance too.

Ask yourself what is the good of this thing to which you are devoting yourself at present.

If the benefit appears limited in any way, appeal to the good in all to show you how to live beyond the limits.

Look out.

*See what the situation demands, and
if you can't think where to begin,
start with the nearest thing to hand.*

*Don't bother with all those
deep-rooted ideas you hold about yourself.*

*How can you make the best of what's
on offer now when it's peered at
through a screen of self-concern?*

What are you serving at present —
yourself or the situation before you?

One leads to separation, the other
to greater awareness and a more
creative approach to life.

Regardless of what use you make of life,
it is a great grace.

One of the best ways to recognise this
is to live in the awareness of the
three graces of beauty, love and joy.

See beauty, give love, experience joy.

If what you are meeting appears to be nothing out of the ordinary, look again.

The Time of Your Life

The great thing about the present moment is that it is the only time that we are truly alive. But, so busy are we preparing to live at some other time, we miss this obvious fact.

The experience of what is currently on offer is so often overlaid with preoccupations, distractions, fear and expectation, and yet it is only in the present that genuine concerns can be met with any understanding. It is only in the present that things can be timed to perfection, tackled with a touch of true artistry.

Every other way of working must be dull by comparison. This is self-evident. Yet emotional involvement has its way of possessing heart and mind, and methods have to be consciously adopted to realign our perception and connect with the present.

The reflections contained in this chapter are designed to bring the mind back from the concerns for the past and the future. They allow you to become aware of what 'now' might offer and to discover the time of your life in all its fullness and power.

True knowledge arises from experience, not information.

Gather the knowledge needed in the only time possible.

Make sure you haven't overlooked the obvious.

*Make sure you haven't
overlooked the obvious.*

Look again. Think again.

Think about what's happening to you now.

What do you really need to know?

What are you being told by the circumstances you face?

*Understanding meets you
moment by moment.*

Make sure you're there when it happens.

*The more alert we are to the
moment the more time expands.*

Give yourself time by developing awareness.

When you face the flow of life,
find your pleasure in what the
moment offers, but when the moment
has passed, simply let it go.

What is it that cuts you off from the present, and in the process what are you missing out on?

Ask yourself this question:
What is the world for me now?

If it is a small and narrow place,
go beyond.

Step out into the open, right now.

*There is no other life than the life
that is being lived now.*

Freedom lies in being there when it happens.

*Look for the perfection in the
present moment.*

Be wise now, not at some other time, even if 'now' doesn't appear too encouraging.

*In the present there is no time for
worrying about petty concerns.*

*Worry and concern occur when you
project the past into the future.*

Who knows what tomorrow might bring?

Now is the time for opportunity.

Finding Freedom

All of us are confined by our circumstances in life, some dramatically so, and yet freedom can always be availed. This freedom is brought about not so much by changing our outer circumstances, but by discovering freedom of mind.

There is the outer world and all the events we meet, and there is the inner world by means of which we see that outer world.

Much more than our outer circumstances, it is our confining thoughts and feelings which create our experience of life. The reflections in this chapter provide us with a key to unlock those confines which habitually hem us in. They allow us to meet events in an entirely new way, creatively and responsively, with spontaneity and freedom.

*Observe the sort of things that box
you in: thinking about the same old
things, sucked in by familiar desires,
responding in the same old way,
ruled by the usual states of mind.*

*When you see these things predominating,
don't automatically believe they're true.*

Lift your mind above confining thought.

Look up.

See the beauty and seek the simple solution.

Are you really awake at present?

How keenly do you appreciate things?

What can you do to make a step towards greater awareness at present, right now?

*The quality of the decisions we make
is dependent on the degree of
consciousness we bring to them.*

*Regardless of our limitations,
remember that within us all is the
source of perfect freedom.*

*Consciously turn to that before
making decisions.*

Use the exercise of Self-Remembering.

Use it in the here and now.

Use it to step back from the immediate emotional involvement.

Use it to see the matter clearly.

Allow your own light to brighten your mind.

*When there's greater understanding
our limitations dissolve.*

*Likewise, when we go beyond our
limited way of thinking so we gain
a greater understanding of ourselves.*

*Use that understanding to
understand others.*

The future never comes.

Now is our only opportunity.

When confined by heart and mind
remember there's only one opportunity
and only one time.

*The more we are partial to,
the more we dismiss.*

*The more we dismiss, the more we
become isolated from the whole.*

*What in the end we are left with might not
amount to very much, but at least we have
control over our small corner, or so we
think, despite evidence to the contrary.*

When you are stuck with the same old set of thoughts going round and round in your mind, why go with them?

Why not connect with what the moment is asking of you?

Take pleasure in responding to that.

Observation, formulation, application.

Use these three when developing a more philosophical approach to life.

Build on your insights rather than allowing them to be forgotten amidst the usual habits of mind.

The Beauty of It All

I f we were ever to set out to discover beauty, we wouldn't have far to go. The great thing about nature is that it is, by nature, beautiful – everything about it – and nature surrounds us everywhere.

The only thing that stands in the way of a total recognition of this obvious fact is what we put up to prevent it.

But just in the same way that, by simply giving our attention to listening and looking, hearing can be sharpened and sight made more acute, so insight can be developed to make us aware of the presence of beauty everywhere.

What must be understood is that the outer beauty of the world could not be recognised by us if we didn't have inner beauty. One rises to meet the other, but only if what stand in between – our habits of mind – are removed. This is how insight is developed.

The reflections in this chapter encourage a rise in consciousness. They give us a sense of our own inner beauty and grant us the open heart which allows us to recognise and employ the creative flow of life.

Don't dismiss anything as unworthy.

*At heart, everything has its
own peculiar charm.*

The awareness of beauty leads to serenity of mind, and serenity of mind leads to a deeper appreciation of beauty.

One leads naturally to the other.

You can always be in conflict, or you can discover balance and harmony.

They can only be found through stillness.

Constantly come back to that.

And having found it, look again.

Beauty heals.

*Constantly return to the power of beauty,
however it might manifest, as a healing
factor for heart and mind.*

*Carry something of beauty with
you as a reminder.*

Return to it constantly.

*Don't lose touch with the
wonder of things.*

*By seeing this world as
something merely material,
the magic is lost.*

*Things look beautiful because
the mind is beautiful.*

*Therefore, every time you recognise
the beauty without, you meet
the beauty within.*

*What is it about those people who may
not have physical beauty but have
discovered beauty in the way they live?*

What is it they possess?

Become aware of beauty, not possessed by this or that beautiful thing, but as a spirit permeating everything.

*Avoid covering the things you meet
with a quick glance of recognition.*

Look instead with the eyes of an artist.

Take delight in colour and form.

Nothing is ever the same.

Vital Mind, Vital Body

There are times when we feel vitally alive, ready and willing to cope with any demand life presents. At other times, however, accessing the energy we once possessed seems an utter impossibility. This may not have much to do with our physical condition, but more with our state of mind. Those negative thoughts and feelings that can so easily go to create the usual way we deal with things do nothing but drain us of our power.

Under these circumstances what is needed is a change of mind, a new way of meeting events. This way has everything to do with self-discovery, with developing more than a surface response to life. It is to do with training our hearts and minds to make connection with our real selves, our own source of creative energy, and learning to act from that.

To re-energise mind and body we must re-educate our thinking. Turn to the constantly new rather than the old habits of thought that do nothing but wear us down.

Use the reflections in this chapter to unlock your own creative core and tap the vitality to be found there.

*Consider those habits of mind that are
life-enhancing and those that
are energy-destroying.*

*Ask yourself what you're encouraging at
present and what effect this has on others.*

When the mind is dull and heavy and the heart is cold and closed, don't think that this is who you really are.

Your power is a quiet presence lying behind all this.

Everything by nature runs down.

That's true for us as for everything else.

Conscious effort is the only thing that will halt the decline in consciousness.

Find vitality by finding yourself.

Practise Self-Remembering.

*The energy you are empowered
by manifests now.*

The past is full of exhausted energy.

*Check where your mind is tending, and
constantly return to where power is found.*

How do you engage with life?

Is it a productive relationship?

*When you greet life with enthusiasm,
what do you receive?*

By fuelling negative emotion with our own vitality, what we create is nothing but debility.

Notice the inevitable effect of your companions, and this goes for your thoughts and feelings as well as the friends you keep.

If your experience of life lacks life,
seek signs of life in all that
surrounds you everywhere.

This is your life too.

When the fabric of our lives is woven of desire and dislike, notice how ragged and worn out we can easily become.

There's the running around kind of energy, so often uneconomic and wasteful, and there is the intelligent kind which arises from stillness to meet the need and then goes back from where it came.

This is power with purpose.

Living Beyond the Limits

O ur limits are only too obvious. We are limited creatures possessing a limited life, in touch with a limited circle of friends we haven't time for because time is short. Our limited intelligence limits our understanding. What understanding we do possess is penned in by all the limited thinking forced on us by society. We are confined by our circumstances and the demands of others, and after we have exhausted our limited vitality we die and dissolve into dust.

It's so easy to slip into this way of thinking. Even so, all of us have had some experience of something within us that lies beyond all these apparent limitations, something to which even limited access would allow us an altogether more unlimited approach to life, allow us to meet the moment free from the usual constraints, free to act spontaneously, in accord with the need of the situation: something that would give to all our limited circumstances a touch of the limitless.

Use these reflections to go beyond the usual limits.

Will all those things which concern you now go on concerning you for evermore?

Or are they matters which, though important, are bound to pass?

Claim nothing.

Enjoy.

Develop peace in action.

Find the still point even in the midst of turmoil.

This is the best way to step free of anxiety and stress.

*Be sure that you have given
yourself time and space.*

*Avoid the temptation of rushing
in and filling it up.*

*Find space, give space, and from this space
allow the truly creative to arise.*

Integration takes place when the limited joyfully recognises and willingly returns to the unlimited whole.

Any move towards unity must have its effects.

Don't keep yourself separate.

Make the first step.

We never experience happiness in isolation.

When the mind becomes still and reflective what we are experiencing is a reality which goes beyond any self-imposed limits.

Let your dimension be dictated by what's demanded of you.

Rise to the occasion, whatever the occasion might be.

Are we to wait for the great and glorious
or will the everyday do just as well?

Such is the unified nature of things,
what truly benefits us must benefit all.

It cannot be otherwise.

Anything else is no benefit at all.

Cultivate wonder.

To be full of wonder means to stand in awe.

Awe is what we experience when we are faced with that which is unbounded by limits.

And yet where are we to discover this wonder but in that confined thing that stands before us now?

Look beyond the limits.

Timeless Moments

It's so easy to live a boring, humdrum existence. It requires no special effort. All that it needs is for us to stick with the habitual, and make no attempt to open our minds to what lies beyond, certainly to make no attempt to savour the joy of life, to appreciate its potent simplicity, its fullness and depth.

Such a way of living is easy but unsatisfying. What encourages dissatisfaction is the memory that we all carry of something beyond the usual experience, a place where we might get in touch with our true vitality and certain happiness.

In timeless moments we discover ourselves. These timeless moments speak of knowledge, consciousness and bliss, the eternal powers, and we, being born into the framework of time, can only come to experience them in timeless moments.

There's only one time to experience these timeless moments, full of the potency of these powers. Now. Don't give up on the present. Constantly go back to where you might meet what all truly desire. Use these reflections to strengthen that resolve.

Every moment is special.

Learn to look at each seemingly mundane moment as something entirely unusual, as indeed it is.

*It's impossible to discover anything
at any other time but now.*

It's the time for understanding.

*Whatever you may carry in your
heart, meet the moment anew.*

The best way to hide what you really know is to make up your mind before you begin.

Trying to grasp at past happiness is a sure way of losing what's presently on offer.

Why not check to see what it might be.

Devote yourself to the present.

And by doing so discover the eternal powers that can exist at no other time.

Come into the present and revitalise life.

*Although we live in the field of time,
moment by moment, eternally present, are
the vital principles of beauty, love and joy.*

*To discover anything about their nature,
return to where they are found, the present.*

When we begin to submit to the universal powers within us we cannot help but be empowered by their presence for the good of all.

Take time out to discover them.

*Depth of understanding, depth of insight
requires you to enter both more deeply into
the situation before you, and more deeply
into your own depth and stillness.*

Do both. Look out. Look in.

There's no such thing as an old flame.

Love can't be imported from the past.

There's only one time to love.

Learn to love life at the time life lives.

That which is truly beautiful must possess something of the infinite nature of beauty.

Constantly return to when the infinite is expressed: now.

Eternal ideals aren't distant things but pressing matters.

Contained in what presents itself at present, whatever it might be, is your connection with the eternal.

Lasting Relationships

I t can appear that little remains constant in the
passage of time. Change is inevitable. There are
obvious stages in life. We grow and develop in all
kinds of ways. Opportunities arise and must be
seized. We may constantly move on in our desire to
enrich our lives, to gain something greater. This is all
understandable, especially when we look round and
see that the one thing certain in life is that nothing
remains the same.

Yet despite this constant change there is that in us
that yearns for stability, continuity and something
upon which we may rely. The great ideal of
friendship is that you can always turn to a friend.
The great ideal of family is that it's always there for
you and has been for generations. At the heart of the
family lies love, and it's a kind of love that makes for
true friendship.

In these relationships we give and we receive. Lasting
relationships grow in depth because the continuing
journey of discovery embarked on by those involved
in fruitful lives is undertaken in the company of
family and friends.

The most potent of all the powers we possess is the capacity to love. Without it, does life have any real purpose? And no one ever loved alone. Use the reflections in this chapter to help strengthen what you already have and to forge new and lasting relationships.

For the spirit of love to remain as the true dynamic in your life it needs to be served.

Would you stick around if totally ignored?

Serve love.

*When you feel your heart growing hard
seek ways of showing compassion.*

*Approach things with care
and understanding.*

*Give the very thing that you have
lost in yourself.*

*Constantly celebrate the good
qualities of those you love.*

Praise them, both in mind and aloud.

There is consuming desire and lasting love.

*The one is confined, the
other ever expansive.*

Be aware of the atmosphere around you.

*Are you surrounded by ease and
content or something more complicated
and manipulative?*

There is giving or self-seeking.

*How can people living their independent
lives, each pursuing their personal
desires hope to unite in love?*

Love is an eternal principle.

It is not a fleeting experience.

*Lasting relationships are the means we have
been given of serving that principle, always.*

The healing element in life is love.

Give of yourself in the spirit of love
in order to heal perceived wrong.

*In your relationships ask what lies
in between the two of you.*

*If it is full of pitfalls and traps ask
yourself if you are the one who's
creating them and if so, why.*

*Be constant, and in so doing remain true
both to those you love and to yourself.*

From Strength to Strength

There are times when the normal confines we work within give way to something greater. It would appear that we have a power within us that is unlocked either by the demands of the moment or just by the joy of being alive. We possess a new-found vitality, a strength to take on things that were previously beyond us.

This is what we know before our habitual framework of thought closes in and the energy drains away and we go back to feeding on things which weaken rather than confirm our strength.

There is an answer to this: believe in what you experience in those times of power rather than in the opinion you have trained your mind to accept. Feed on things which encourage that strength to grow. Then go on to gather more by giving to others what you have gained for yourself. This is going from strength to strength, and it doesn't stop at personal empowerment for, by reclaiming your own strength, you help others reclaim theirs.

Use the reflections in this chapter to connect with your own inner strength and, by recognising your own power, allow others to recognise theirs.

*Don't search around for something
to lean on, lean on yourself.*

Come to stillness.

*Let go of mental agitation and physical
tensions — draw breath, draw strength.*

The occasional flash of brilliance will not grant you the strength you need, nor the occasional effort.

Regular input is what's required.

Keep practising.

*You can't gather strength when what
you feed mind and body on is bound
to weaken them both.*

*The next time you feel drained go back and
see what you've been doing with yourself,
where you've been letting the mind tend
and what emotions you've given way to.*

Likewise strengthen strength.

When the energy is flowing, assess the factors that have allowed that flow: your state of heart and mind.

*Develop strategies that encourage
the sustaining of energy.*

*Then avoid exceeding the natural measure
by expending energy in useless activity.*

*When the task is done,
return the energy to stillness.*

The worst and most destructive way of expending energy is by deliberately harbouring negative emotion.

Whenever you experience anger or frustration, jealousy or resentment — regardless of how justified you feel — simply let them go.

*Life can so easily turn into
one long jumble.*

*Punctuate events with the
practice of Self-Remembering.*

Create a break in the onward rush.

*Return to rest before turning
to the next thing.*

Neither rush out nor sink back, but instead seek the natural measure in any activity by regular practice of Self-Remembering.

Constantly return to where the exuberance of life is to be discovered — your own still source of power.

And when the time for action is over,
leave it.

Cool analysis is one thing, running
action replays is quite another.

*Vague wishes are quite different
from determined action.*

*One can leave you with nothing but a sense
of uselessness and nagging frustration, the
other of purpose and true satisfaction.*

*One debilitates, the other offers
yet more strength.*

Life Achievement

We have been born as human beings with all the powers humans possess. This is an achievement in itself. It may not appear to be anything to do with any personal effort we may have made. To us has been freely given the gift of life. When we consider all the things we would like to achieve we must hold in mind what we were given at the beginning – that thing without which nothing could be done. To remain true to that must involve us in making good use of these miraculous tools of mind and body. It would be absurd to think that we were given them merely to squander.

The desire to give of ourselves in the same measure as it has been given would provide a firm basis for life's true achievement.

Use what is to be found in this chapter to make creative use of the gifts you have been given; in the process discover your unique purpose, that which is yours alone to fulfil.

*Taking the initiative involves you in
seizing the opportunities that come your
way rather than rejecting your chances,
failing to act when action is needed,
letting the moment pass.*

*Taking the initiative involves you in
doing what has been given to you to do,
using your own particular gifts,
rather than living a life of dissatisfaction,
jealous of others' achievements.*

When habits of mind lower your sights, don't give way to them.

Seek the creative solution rather than the one that habits of mind seem to dictate.

*Work to retain that freshness of view
which you were given when the
gift of life was new.*

Look as if for the first time.

Don't fall back on the accepted patterns.

The truly creative must be new.

It's not so much the sudden insights and brilliance that tend to control our lives.

Habits of mind are the big thing.

Examine yourself.

Separate good from bad, and develop your strengths with persistence and method.

*If your mind automatically turns
to negative emotions, refuse to
place your belief in them.*

*Who would trust those things that
persistently undermine achievement?*

Identify your true desires, ones that will grant you proper fulfilment, ultimate satisfaction.

When in touch with these, the strength will be given and real enthusiasm.

For the true and fundamental desires must in some way serve the greater good.

And of the greater good there is no limit.

*Always seek the measured response,
just sufficient to resolve the need,
however that need might show itself.*

Anything less will not suffice.

*Anything more will bring with
it unnecessary complications.*

Adopt measure.

Work from stillness not agitation.

Work from harmony not discord.

*Use the practice of Self-Remembering
to find both.*

*Your achievements will inevitably
carry with them the qualities that they
were originally conceived with.*

Recognise mind and body as exquisite tools.

*Like any precision instrument they need
to be treated with care and respect.*

*You must constantly bring them
back to balance and harmony.*

Resolve tension.

Learn to love doing it by doing it for the love of it, whatever it might be.

Lasting achievements are pursued with passion and steady resolution.

Final Thought

*Vital in the outward thrust of life,
calm within, all desire to possess these
wonderful gifts, for they change everything.*

The use of these reflections leads you on a path of self-knowledge, understanding and certainty, all of which enable you to meet the demands of life with a new source of creative energy.

Return to what is to be found in this book over and over again. Put the reflections to the test in all the situations you meet.

What is wisdom after all but discovery in experience? What is the only change worth making but for the better?

Be reflective.

Use reason.

Live consciously.